God Loves Salespeople

AN INSPIRATIONAL BOOK TO GET WHAT YOU WANT IN LIFE

By Amani S. Ahmed

Copyright © 2018 Amani S. Ahmed

All rights reserved. No part of this book may be used or reproduced by any means, graphic, electronic, or mechanical, including photocopying, recording, taping, or by any information storage retrieval system, without the written permission of the publisher except in the case of brief quotations embodied in critical articles and reviews.

The intent of the author is only to offer general information to help you in your quest for emotional and spiritual welfare. In the event you use any of the information in this book for yourself or others, the author and the publisher assume no responsibility for your actions.

ISBN 10: 1-68411-580-9
ISBN 13: 978-1-68411-580-8

ALSO BY AMANI S. AHMED

Master Your Mind: Activate The Power Within You And Change Your Life

A Beginner's Guide To Abundant Living

The 3 D's To Life: A Simple Guide To Unlocking Your True Power

All of the above may be ordered online by visiting: www.iamworthyinc.com

This Book Is Dedicated To...

My wonderful husband and sons. My loving mother, dad, nieces, nephews, and sisters, including Ghada who is in Heaven.

I dedicate this book to all that are seeking freedom from the traditional way of living. Yearning to live in God's Truth of freedom and joy.

This book is dedicated and made ONLY for you!

Thank you GOD for your grace and insight to write such a powerful and life changing book.

Love,
Amani

Contents

INTRODUCTION 1

CHAPTER ONE 4
   Be The Landlord Of Your Beliefs 4

CHAPTER TWO 11
   Understanding Your Beliefs 11

CHAPTER THREE 21
   What Doesn't Serve You Can't Make You Stronger ... 21

CHAPTER FOUR 34
   The Problem & The Solution 34

CHAPTER FIVE 50
   Building Self Confidence To Make Your Dreams A Reality 50

CHAPTER SIX 65
   You And God: The Premise 65

CHAPTER SEVEN 80
   Choosing God's Will Over All Else 80

CHAPTER EIGHT 96
   God Is A Yes For Your Dreams And Desires, Launch Them 96

CONCLUSION 103

About The Author 108

INTRODUCTION

God loves salespeople because this is the only kind of person that needs to be present to make something happen. Try selling half asleep. The best speakers, trainers, musicians, artists, and world leaders are most present.

We have made many advances in today's world. We have come a long way from the days of horse and buggies thus we now live in one of the most advanced civilizations the world has ever known. Today, we have higher buildings and wider roads, but shorter temperaments and narrower points of view. We spend more but enjoy it less.

We have bigger houses, but smaller families, more free time, but we spend less of it with the people who are most valuable to us. We reached the Moon and came back, but we find it troublesome to cross our own street and meet our neighbors. We have conquered the outer space, but not our inner space.

These are the times of finer houses, but broken homes. Even with all the advances mankind has made, we have forgotten what is important. In our rush to improve our standard of living, materially, we have forgotten the spiritual side of our lives.

We now are beginning to see some serious problems developing because we, as a society, have forgotten what is important. The moral breakdowns that began in the 60s are now taking a tremendous toll on our way of life. It is way past time to get back to the basics of life and follow the age-old concepts that enabled us to reach this high level of success.

In today's world, what is right is wrong, and what is wrong is right, many people have forgotten or never been taught the common sense values that continue to work for generation after generation.

Many people think that just because they believe something, or because some influential person in their life told them something, it is true. One might have been able to rely on the wisdom of others in the past; however, today, that simply isn't true.

What was common sense and wisdom only a few short years ago, is now thought to be extremism by many in today's society. Try to inform people of values that work and many times you will be ridiculed for being a nut job and half crazy.

The only way for us, as a society, to recover from this debacle is for the people who still remember what the time-tested values were to cling to their guns and supreme manuals. We have been silent for too long. We need to speak out, facing ridicule is a minor inconvenience compared to what we will face if society doesn't get back doing the things that work, instead of following the latest trend out of Hollywood.

Just seeing what kind of lives most of those people lead should be enough to convince us that the correct path in life is doing just the opposite of what they do.

Now is the time to stand firm in our beliefs, it is the only way out of this mess.

God loves salespeople, we are bombarded by so many choices and have endless possibilities. The one that exceeds in life is the one that sells most people on their ideas.

CHAPTER ONE

Be The Landlord Of Your Beliefs

When you think of a top selling person- what do they possess? A firm belief in an idea.

Beliefs are an interesting thing. They aren't there from the day you are born. They are gradually passed on to you by your parents based on their lives and experiences. These beliefs are for them a way of thinking - a way of life. They take them for granted as fact for your safety.

Without knowing any different, we take on and follow these beliefs. After all, our surroundings and environment are supporting these beliefs so there's every reason to begin to support them ourselves.

As you grow older and begin to socialize, you are potentially exposed to a wider range of beliefs. Some of these new beliefs may be in conflict or different to what you have taken on as your own, and some may also be the same or similar to what you have come to believe and accept as true.

So, what is a belief? If you were to break it right down, a belief is a convenient assumption that something is true or false. Quite often, people mix up beliefs as facts.

This can be simply illustrated by a familiar scenario.

Let's say there are 2 cars that smash on a suburban street, one is a red car and the other is a blue car. These are the facts - irrefutable and undeniable. Let's say there are a couple of witnesses including the driver of each car. One person says that the driver of the red car is at fault, while another says the blue car did the wrong thing. The driver of the red car complains that the blue car didn't give way for a sufficient amount of time which caused the accident. The driver of the blue car says that the red car was going too fast, which caused the accident. The differences in these stories all come back to beliefs. Believing what is seen from the angle that we see it.

Beliefs are a powerful thing, but more importantly and may be difficult for some to swallow - beliefs are not real. Beliefs are completely made up. Remember, a belief is a convenient assumption that something is true or false. And we have a belief for everything - and I mean everything.

We are very quickly able to assess any situation that we meet by running it through our "belief filter". In milliseconds, we can choose whether something fits within our belief system or not. Even if it's something completely foreign to us, we are able to make an almost immediate assessment and create a belief in it. We instantly call upon reference points from our surroundings, our past, and our peers - anything, so we can create a belief that makes sense to us and is congruent to our other beliefs.

When you were younger, there was very little to question in regards to our beliefs. They were generally there to keep us safe or to help us grow. But some beliefs have an expiry date and are no longer valid or useful.

I'm presuming that those that are reading this are adults and, therefore, I can safely talk about the belief in Santa Claus (fingers crossed...). This is a belief that a lot of people are familiar with, and has been used by many families for generations. Some will defend it and some will tell you that it's lying to children. Those conversations are all based on beliefs! But the point I wanted to make by bringing it up here, is that there is a point that parents generally reach where they feel that this belief has reached its expiration date - that the child is "old enough to know the truth".

I'm not going to enter the conversation as to whether I think it is helpful or not to indulge in this belief - that's for you to decide. But it's a perfect example of assessing and deciding whether a belief serves or hinders.

There are beliefs that served us at one particular point in our lives that we have carried around far longer than we have needed to. There are also beliefs that we have created that have never actually been a healthy choice but were made to get through a specific time because we thought it would help.

Are the beliefs that you hold on to and live by helping you today?

Are any of them holding you back from something far greater than you could experience?

Are any of your beliefs created based on fear?

Do you still hold on to a belief that worked for you when you were younger, but is redundant today?

These types of questions are ones that we should be asking of each and every one of our beliefs. Whenever something comes up, ask yourself, "Is this belief helping me, or hurting me?" It's not enough to just answer yes or no; you must then justify to yourself why you have given the answer that you have given. You will defend your beliefs automatically, so it is important to justify their existence.

Remember that you have spent many years living with some beliefs - yet, they are merely tenants. There are tenants that will leave a place spick and span, and there are tenants that will trash a place with little regard for anything or anyone.

Become the property manager of your beliefs - do regular inspections. See whether your tenants are keeping the place neat and tidy. If one of these tenants is no longer suitable to live there, then it's easy enough to replace them with another resident that will be suitable.

You are the landlord of your beliefs. You hold the deed. You are where they reside. Are you deciding the terms of the tenancy, or are they?

The day you decide to take control of your beliefs and really size up what is helpful to you and what is not, you will create a major change in your life. Once you rid yourself of the beliefs that are no longer of service to you, you will find yourself replacing old beliefs with ones that invigorate and inspire you into positive action.

A belief's job is there to serve you and the world around you. If a belief causes you to blame, hold you back from pursuing your ideal life then it has no place in your life anymore. If a belief causes you to harm yourself or others in any way, it has no place in your life. Although beliefs themselves aren't real, the effects that they have on us and our surroundings are very real.

Size up your beliefs. Be the landlord and property manager of your beliefs and conduct regular inspections. Assess whether they are keeping the place tidy or are taking advantage of you and making a mess of things.

Once you decide to take control and evict those bad tenants from your life to replace with good ones, you will immediately experience a positive change.

And make no mistake - the old tenants will bang on the door complaining that they've been loyal residents for years and years. They'll tell you that they've kept you safe from a bunch of bad things, but what they won't tell you as they try to get back in is all the good things that they've stopped you from experiencing. They won't tell you about all the pain they've caused while being a resident.

They won't tell you about the lost opportunities that their existence has caused you to miss. They won't tell you the hurt they've caused you, your family or friends.

They'll lie to get back in the door. Don't trust them. You've asked the right questions, you know that they aren't suitable tenants. There's a list of good tenants patiently waiting for you to give them a place to stay. All you have to do is make room for them.

At the end of the day, a belief is either helping or hurting, and being that they are made up, I recommend choosing beliefs that are there to help you and those around you.

Do your homework, and choose your tenant wisely. Your dreams are possible regardless of what your mind or ego says.

CHAPTER TWO

Understanding Your Beliefs

How would you know that the beliefs you have about yourself, how the world is and your reason for existence are true? Now, I completely agree that these are some pretty big questions to ponder over, but have you ever stopped for long enough to consider why you believe the things that you do? Have you ever questioned where your beliefs came from? How they got there? Are they even true?

Have you ever questioned or doubted them? Evaluated, assessed or critiqued them? Have you ever even resented them? How do you know what the beliefs you hold about yourself are? Or has someone else just decided them for you? Did you choose your beliefs intentionally? Did you learn them via the stories you've told yourself in relation to your experiences? Have you adopted them by carefully modeling someone that you have utmost trust and respect for? Or has it just been the case that you had a whole load of opinions and statements rammed down your throat by one of your parents, a teacher or authority figure who played a role in your life somewhere in the past?

Do the beliefs that you have about yourself energetically drive you towards achieving great and wonderful things or would you be able to recognize if they'd keep you trapped in small thinking, doom, and gloom about your future, mediocrity, and misery?

Do these beliefs serve you, or are you just a slave to them? Are you really in control of your life or are you just caught in the current and swept along with whatever makes you happy?

ARE ALL BELIEFS LIMITING BELIEFS?

Do your beliefs help you get closer towards fulfilling the dreams and goals you have for your life, or do they keep you in your own private mental and emotional prison?

I once heard a story from a guy that used to go visit an inmate in prison. I was told about an inmate of the prison who had millions of pounds stashed away somewhere, waiting for him after his 12-year sentence for committing counterfeit fraud! Now, although his family were quite financially affluent who live in a nice house, in a nice area with kids who went to the best schools and colleges - this family was minus a husband and father. A high price to pay for financial security I'd suggest?

As we consider this story though, imagine if we were to go into the big city, and visit a highly successful law practice where the new guys are earning at least $100,000 a year, and the company partners are in a financial position where they could have stopped working years ago!

These inner city lawyers will work very long days, weekends, and even evenings, with rooms inside of their corporate offices, which serve them like a home away from home.

They only see their kids for a couple of hours each week - if they're even married anymore and their wives haven't already divorced them!

You may be able to identify the differences in these men's lives through; where one is currently serving a 12-year sentence in a prison (most likely against his free will), whereas the other is serving a life sentence in an inner city law practice! I guess that although the lawyer might get to exercise his freedom a little more often, he's likely to be in his prison for 40 years, not just 12 years like the comparative inmate who even stands to qualify for early release!

Is this how people truly want to live? Or do we all just live incongruently to our beliefs about whom it is that we are, and how the world around us works?

Some of the world's greatest architects might suggest that the greatest prisons are those that have been built of cast iron, reinforcement, and concrete. However, I'm going to suggest that the most enslaving prison man can be kept in - is the prison of his own mind, the prison of his beliefs, the limitations of his thinking, and the nature of his own relative subjectivity.

So, turning the focus back on you... do your beliefs enable you to explore your fullest potential and do truly amazing things with your life, or have they just kept you imprisoned in a safe, familiar and highly predictable little box where as long as you simply keep on doing what you're doing, you always get what you've always got?

Have your beliefs enabled you to view life clearly and objectively or have they just reminded you of all your past failures and imperfections in a way that fully justifies a small and risk-free approach to life? Have you found your beliefs to be flexible in any way and subject to change depending on your daily experiences and life lessons? Or are they set in concrete where you're not willing to budge an inch and even consider that there is any degree of truth outside of the extent of your own life experiences?

What would happen, if one day you were to wake up and discover that everything that you've believed to be true about your life, was completely untrue? Have you ever considered what it would be like for you if you were to begin living your life with a completely different set of beliefs? Would it be better? Would it be worse? Would you begin doing things differently? What if you questioned every belief you have about yourself and life? That's why I say don't believe what you believe.

Have you ever (even for a moment) considered the possibility that perhaps some of your longest serving and most non-negotiable beliefs could be completely untrue? What would it mean if, for your whole life, you had gotten the completely wrong end of the stick and had grown to believe a whole lot of things about the world, that were completely untrue?

"Our ability to change a belief will be hugely determined by our level of emotional investment in the particular subject that our belief is about." Kain Ramsay

What I'm saying here is that there are certain beliefs that we desperately want to be true (even if they're false) and so if we're presented with new information that either challenges or contradicts our beliefs, then we'll be likely to react negatively and sometimes even completely irrationally.

SO WHERE DO OUR BELIEFS COME FROM?

1. *Our Influences:* From the moment we're born, we are bombarded with information from a myriad of sources. Our beliefs are often heavily influenced by the people in our world - especially those closest to us. Our mind is constantly absorbing, interpreting, filtering and processing information. Much of what we absorb in a day happens without our conscious awareness; it happens despite us. From infancy, our parents, friends, teachers, our heroes, the TV we watch, the music we listen to, the books we read and even the websites we frequent, have influenced us to think and believe a certain way. If you grew up in an environment that taught you education is paramount to your success in life, you'll be likely to

demand that your kids finish school, get the best exam grades, and go off to further education.

2. *Our Experiences:* What happens to us, teaches us. Some of us see ourselves as victims when we're actually not. We all have an amazing capacity to learn, but most of our learning happens unconsciously and unintentionally. Sadly, not all of our "lessons" empower us or put us in a better place. Some of our lessons teach us that we're stupid, ugly, undesirable or incapable. Some experiences are the basis for many of our disempowering (or totally debilitating) beliefs. For many of us to move forward and into a better place (mentally, emotionally, physically, practically), we need to unlearn much of what we've made "truth" in our world. That is, we need to change our beliefs.

When you come into the world, you are a big (or little) blank slate with certain inherited attributes, instincts and reflexes like eating, breathing, and reflexes. These are the things that are stored in your basic human nature (your pre-programming). As you journey through life, you form habits, beliefs, and values based on your interpretation of your life's experiences. This kind of makes you the expert at just being you!

These beliefs, values, and habits will have been determined and underpinned by your experience of culture, your parents, your friends, television, music genres, books, the propaganda of politicians and your own assumptions, judgments, and complete misunderstandings. Once a belief is formed, any information from these sources is filtered so that you can strengthen and validate your original belief and reject any information that might contradict it (it's not like you'd go out of your way to prove yourself wrong, would you!) For example, if you believe that you are ugly, stupid, incompetent or useless, there would be no amount of reassurance from friends or family that would make you feel better, because you'd reject any new information that acts contradictory to whatever it is that you believe.

HOW MANY DIFFERENT TYPES OF BELIEFS ARE THERE?

Over the years, beliefs have been classified in various ways by various people; however, I'm going to attempt to simplify and lose the theological psycho-babble that's often found in textbooks because I don't fully understand what half of the long words mean! For practical reasons, I will break beliefs down into three simple categories:

1. *Positive Beliefs-* these are beliefs that enable us to maintain a helpful, positive, productive, creative and empowered headspace that allows us to explore and fulfill our fullest potential. These are the beliefs that pull us through life's tough times, they allow us to deal with our fears and ultimately come out the other side of them much stronger, wiser and far better equipped.

2. *Negative Beliefs-* obviously, the polar opposite of the positive kind! They will destroy your potential, your happiness, your relationships, your career, your confidence, your mental health and your life... if you allow them to!

3. *Circumstantial Beliefs-* these beliefs are exactly as they sound; not typically life-altering or changing in any way, just there. For example; I believe that Paris is a great place to live. I believe the sun will come up tomorrow morning and that rowing is one of the most effective cardio workouts that a human being can do! We have thousands of these types of belief that just exist somewhere in the recesses of our brains and don't really serve a greater meaning or purpose other than to give us a difference of opinion from others.

The human mind can be our very own worst enemy with its self-defeating conversations matched up with what's often a very limited understanding of how we can most effectively pursue the things that we want most in life.

There was this ancient Greek Philosopher called Plato, who over 1500 years ago made an interesting statement in one of the things that we can often value the most in life. Our opinions! Plato claimed that, "Opinion, is nothing more than the medium between certainty and complete ignorance", which may or may not have completely undermined many of the bold and courageous statements that other philosophers, religious leaders, intellects and many of those in the education establishments have committed their lives to believing for centuries beforehand.

I guess that what Plato was trying to highlight here, is that our opinions about things are nothing more than circumstantial beliefs!

CHAPTER THREE

What Doesn't Serve You Can't Make You Stronger

My friend grew up in a Christian home which was regularly frequented by good churchy folks, who attended Christian schools and Christian services where they were taught about life (God, religion, marriage, relationships, sex, good, bad, right, wrong) exclusively from a Christian perspective.

As she grew up, hanging out with her Christian friends and only ever seeing the inside of a Christian church, she was probably never going to become a heavy metal punk rocker or even become a Buddhist by her fifteenth birthday. Her upbringing, her environment, her family and her education taught her that she was born into the one true church. Whatever that was supposed to mean!

She shared with me how as a teenager, she honestly felt sorry for all those non-Christians who were going straight to hell, for hellfire and damnation. Poor buggers! After all, she had the Big J.C. on her team; God's personal representative on planet earth, therefore, how could she ever have possibly gone wrong?

Fortunately for her (as she believed), she had managed to find herself on to the right team - what were the chances!

All those religions to be born into and she was born into the only one that has a hotline to God and obviously the only religion that could get someone into heaven. Talk about luck!

In her early 20's, she went to Bible college where the Senior Pastor told her; "Okay students, we've decided to provide you all with an extensive overview of the core theology, philosophy, and teaching of all the major religions of the world, then we'll leave it up to you to explore the 'God thing' in your own way and see where you land; it's important that you find your own truth, listen to your own heart and develop your own religious and spiritual beliefs and understanding." Oh wait, she wasn't told that at all - they did, after all, want her to join "their" team!

Now, before you begin to think that I'm anti-religious, I'm not. All religions are great! I guess that what I have become very aware of is that there is such a thing as social, emotional and religious conditioning (in any system, organization or religion) that will tell you what to think, how to behave, what's acceptable, what's not acceptable and also what the real truth is that should ultimately be believed.

I'm yet to find an institution in any society that offers any degree of encouragement to explore and discover your own truth beyond the walls of whatever system it is that you find yourself in.

In fact, it's hard to find a single religion, political party or organization which doesn't discourage exploration and free thinking by being critical of groups and individuals who think, believe and behave differently.

The pressure to conform exists in all areas of the human experience way beyond the religions, schools, homes, workplaces, sporting clubs, political parties, street gangs... anywhere where people gather, some form of conformity is required which the social scientists will call cultural expectations (or norms).

You may or may not be able to recognize times in your own life when you've begun to question either the "system" or parts thereof, and have ended up being ridiculed, criticized or even completely rejected by others and labeled as being rebellious, misguided and troublesome.

The reason I'm even talking about my friend's Christian upbringing is because it's been one that has directly impacted me. That's her reference point. Her experience. Her story.

I could just as easily be talking about any system (religious or non religious) that requires people to think, behave and believe a certain way in order to be a "member", where if you don't align with the culturally accepted doctrine, theology, thinking or rules then you can't be part of the group and you just simply won't fit in; therefore, in order to "fit in", you must believe what they believe in the way that they believe whatever it is that they believe.

MANIPULATION IS EVERYWHERE

Everyday, we are constantly being programmed (taught, influenced, impacted and conditioned). Our beliefs are always being molded and manipulated by other people in their attempts to have us "join their team" or to get what they want without us even being aware of it.

Most of our beliefs are formed over many years, which is why they can become such a firmly entrenched and non-negotiable part of our mental and emotional DNA. And a lifetime of being taught a certain message or philosophy can make it extremely difficult for us to consider any other degree of reality other than the one we have already accepted to be true.

When considering to believe anything else other than what we already do, (another version of truth, an alternative option, a new way of living, thinking, seeing or believing) we'll often need to question what it is that we've believed for however long we've been believing it - and this can really take us out of our comfort zones!

THE CULTURE OF A NON-CONFORMIST

Would I even dare to suggest that our own beliefs shouldn't fall into any degree of alignment with a larger group at any time? No, absolutely not. What I will suggest, however, is that in order to live more confident, congruent and genuinely authentic lives, it is vitally important that we learn to discover the difference between our own truth and those belonging to others. In order to become people of value and well-adjusted adults, we must learn our own lessons and determine our own beliefs. Upon doing this, if it so happens that our core beliefs and values happen to align with a group that we want to be a part of, so be it, and that's OK! But simply becoming more aware of when someone else is attempting to hijack our brain and our potential by having us conform to their group's standards and beliefs so that in turn they embrace us. To conform is to compromise and to compromise is to give up our freedom to live with authenticity.

The last thing on my agenda (well, it's actually not on my agenda at all) is to have you pledge your allegiance to my way of thinking. What I would love to achieve through my writings here is for you to become confident enough to thoughtfully consider what I'm discussing. Ponder over what I write, explore it for yourself and carefully contemplate whether this "feels" like "truth" for you. There is a chance that I have wandered so far off the beaten track that I've completely lost my mind and a well-calculated view of what reality even is anymore! If what you're reading right now feels right for you, it's because it probably is. If it feels wrong for you, then it probably is also.

The smartest plan that I'm able to suggest for you in moving your life forward is this: Keep the positive beliefs that serve you and ditch the bad ones that don't!

The only time that you would only ever really consider changing what you believe is when you've reached a stage in your life where something has to give and that things can no longer remain the way that they are. Times like these will generally come to light when a particular belief that you have is outworking itself in some negative way in your life. A belief like this will generally do a pretty good job at capping your potential, limiting your degree of personal or professional productivity, it may have an adverse impact in your relationships, limit your possibilities, your career, the depth of intimacy with your family and even your physical, mental and emotional well-being (often experienced through feeling of low confidence and low self-esteem).

Here are a number of steps that I hope will guide you through this process (and it is a process by the way!)

1. *Become emotionally intelligent:* The greater the degree of emotional investment that we have invested into a certain belief, the more likely it is that we act or behave in a completely irrational, defensive or even a protective way in order to hold onto our belief - even if it has caused us years of unnecessary heartache and pain! The challenge comes in becoming humble enough to simply admit that we may have gotten things wrong! Scary, I know. Deep breaths, you'll be okay.

A great question that we can ask ourselves is, "What do I believe about myself?" but moving beyond this, a more effective question we can ask ourselves is, "Why do I believe what I believe about myself?"

If you are able to honestly answer this question, you have taken one giant leap towards establishing a far greater degree of truth in your life, and I'm quite sure we've all heard the ancient proverb that goes: "... and the Truth will set you free". This truth, whatever it is for you, will set you free in your thinking and your believing, by busting wide open the limiting beliefs that you may or may not have been unnecessarily clinging onto for years.

2. *Feel the fear and do it anyway!* Please apply some logic to this one; I'm not suggesting you go wrestle with a bear or anything here; however, when you summon up the courage to begin working through the challenges you face, you'll have no option other than confronting with and dealing with your fears. This is one of the most effective ways to change the way that you think, what you believe about yourself and ultimately how you behave in relation to the situations and circumstances that you find yourself in.

When you attempt to accomplish something that you may previously believe wasn't even possible for you (such as doing a bungee jump, speaking in public, or forgiving someone for something that doesn't ever warrant forgiveness), not only do you experience a shift in your thinking about that particular achievement, but you also begin questioning any other self-imposed limitations that you've placed upon yourself over the years. When you attempt and complete a challenge that you may never have previously believed to be possible, you open this mental and emotional door which has been shut in your life for way, way too long!

3. *Mix with different types of people.* There's that old saying that, "Birds of a feather, flock together", so, if you've been used to hanging out with judgmental people, negative and paranoid people, miserable or fearful excuse-making people and under-achievers... if you've not already become like these kinds of people, there's a pretty certain chance that you soon will! Who we associate with doesn't necessarily determine who we become in life, but it certainly does influence us.

As much as you're able to, invest your time into building meaningful relationships with people who you admire, respect and even trust; people who will encourage and empower you, not handicap you and hold you back!

4. *Do something different!* If you always do what you've always done, you'll always get what you've always got, and if you always get what you've always got, you'll always have what you've always had! Capiche? Invest time into talking with people you would normally shy away from or those that you may previously have thought that you had nothing in common with. If you don't learn anything new about yourself, that's OK, you will; however, learn more about how these other people have arrived at the life conclusions they have grown to believe. They will teach you something.

I recently had a conversation with an ex-Army guy who was highly critical of a particular religious group. When I asked him which specific parts of their theology, philosophy, and doctrine that he disagreed with, he looked at me blankly. The truth was that he was criticizing something that he didn't fully understand. He'd never read this group's religious texts, or even ever had a meaningful conversation with anyone of that particular faith. After a little probing, I learned that he had simply adopted his beliefs about this group of people from his opinionated and racially intolerant father (who he despised).

5. *Just be you. Stop trying to fit in and people please.* Don't be a brown nose and don't be a sheep. Consistently assess and evaluate the way in which you think, behave and believe today. Explore where your beliefs came from and I can guarantee you that you're venturing out on the journey of a lifetime! Don't adopt mine or anyone else's core beliefs as true because there's a pretty good chance that you don't know how they've come to reach the conclusions that they've reached. Become your own person and make your beliefs your own after you've questioned them, interrogated them, tested them and discovered them to be true for you and you alone.

6. *Re-set the default mode.* Most of us have to work really hard at changing our ways, habits, and beliefs - it's no easy mission! Most of us have an innate tendency to feel that our old beliefs are somehow more real than the new ones we're trying to instill into our mental hard-drives.

If you're like most people then you experience what can feel like a battle going on inside of our mind, between the emotional you with the unhealthy emotional attachments to the old beliefs, behaviors and habits - and rational you who fully understands the implications of what it would mean to just be yourself and be free from the limiting thoughts and beliefs that have plagued you for can often feel like a lifetime.

Replacing old beliefs with new more truthful and empowering ones will enter you into an on-going and life-long process of self-discovery which means that the further you venture down this rabbit hole, the more aware you become of your beliefs and how they impact you in the moment and on a daily basis. This will not be an easy journey; however, I urge and encourage you to take it. Often, you will find yourself having to work hard to over-ride a deep-rooted inner urge to conform to your past pre-existing beliefs, your old ways of thinking, your old ways of doing, your old ways of being, you old ways of reacting, and your old ways of communicating.

The thought of this may scare you, but again I'd urge you to consider the alternate option, change nothing and continue to experience life the exact same way that you always have done. Get the same results. Feel the same feelings and think the same thoughts about yourself.

The choice, my friend, is yours!

In order to create the kind of results that you truly want in this world, you've sometimes got to take a risk. So consider taking the kind of risk that not many people in the world are ever prepared to take for fear of failure, rejection and complete isolation. Just be yourself and believe that you've always been more than enough.

CHAPTER FOUR

The Problem & The Solution

In practically every area of your life, you are the problem and the solution. It may not always seem that way, but you encounter your resistance from the inside, not - as is commonly believed - outside sources. When your subconscious mind accepts new beliefs, whole new realities are suddenly available to you.

As an example, let's say you hold a limiting belief that says, "I find it hard to make new friends", this limiting belief is actually excusing you from making friends, you believe it is not your fault - you just find it hard. Therefore, it is only logical and completely understandable that you don't make friends as your belief deludes you into believing that your lack of friends has nothing to do with you.

But let's say you questioned the belief. Because God's law is that we will experience 100% of what we believe. Can you find examples in your life where you met new people at a family function or a neighborhood watch meeting or a business conference? I'm sure you would agree that you made friends at some time or another.

This was a brave step to test your belief. And you see that it flunked with flying colors. So now what's next. Allow yourself to detach from the current belief no matter how long it has been there and replace it with something else.

If you change your belief to, "I find it easy to make friends ", your diary won't suddenly fill up with new contact details or your telephone won't suddenly start ringing with new appointments, but you will have shifted your focus. Suddenly, the problem is no longer out there, the problem is now with you. In other words, you have now accepted responsibility for your reality and once you have done that, you can begin to examine what you need to change within yourself, and sometimes that simple change of attitude is all you need to open up numerous possibilities.

Now, as you continue with your new belief, that it is easy to make friends, you will suddenly find new evidence to support this, which in turn strengthens your belief even more and you will make whatever changes that are necessary to take full advantage of your newly emerging reality.

Challenge yourself to create new and even more supportive beliefs, even if in the beginning you may not actually believe them on the surface. Constantly remind yourself that you can voluntarily, at will, plant in your subconscious mind any thought, idea or belief you desire, and your mind will accept it provided it is introduced with feeling and reinforced with constant repetition.

You see, the mind is a creature of habit, if you have allowed limiting beliefs and concepts to take root, you can crowd them out by creating new and more supportive beliefs, and by practicing daily until all traces of the old thoughts and beliefs have been completely replaced by the new ones. So do a mental spring-clean, it's time to question then throw away the old limiting, self-defeating beliefs, however much they may be cherished, and replace them.

The following list may be helpful to you, to identify some of your limiting beliefs:-

I can't do it

It won't last

Life is hard

I don't have time

I can't afford it

I'm too young

I'm too old

Nothing is easy

It will never work for me

I never have any good luck

There are no opportunities left

It's not my fault

If any of these sound familiar to you, you must begin immediately to steadfastly imprint new, more positively supportive beliefs.

Allowing ourselves to succeed means being willing to give up the excuses which hold us back and the security and other benefits we have derived from failure. Millions of people are content to stay as they are and will make no attempt to change, despite being unsatisfied with their present situation. They believe that success is destined for somebody else and that it will never happen to them.

They fail to understand that you don't wait for life to happen to you, you make life happen to you by what you believe, and when you are aware of what you believe you can control your own destiny.

So what about you, are you prepared to shake off your old limiting beliefs, are you prepared to ditch your old excuses and assume responsibility for your life? If so then, this book will help you to "Explore Your Possibilities".

HAVE SUCCESSFUL BELIEFS, TO BE SUCCESSFUL!

As we've discussed, beliefs create our reality. We develop beliefs for every area of our life, yet, the most important beliefs that contribute towards our success are the ones that determine the feelings towards oneself. How you view yourself has a direct relationship with the success you will have in the world - if you don't believe you possess value then there is nothing for you to share.

Successful people have successful beliefs. If you need examples for defining a successful belief, I suggest finding people you deem "successful" and ask them, or read biographies from great minds you admire.

If you talk with some of the most successful people in the world, past or present, the most common denominator is related to the goals they set and the beliefs they hold.

God loves salespeople because they go after what they want and have a strong and positive belief in themselves. Hypothetically speaking, if you were God, what would you be saying about your human creations that are always putting themselves down, living afraid, and holding limiting beliefs about themselves? God created us to be independent thinkers, to seek truth for ourselves, and have an undeniable belief in ourself and abilities.

The belief in yourself, your abilities, your value, and your future success is paramount.

Let's dig in.

The power of a belief

"It always seems impossible until it's done." ~ Nelson Mandela

In 1954, the commonly held belief in the world was that it was humanly impossible to run a four-minute mile. That's until Roger Bannister came along, believing and proclaiming he'll do the impossible. Sure enough, after many close attempts, he broke the four-minute barrier by 6 seconds! He shattered people's beliefs by doing the impossible.

Know what happened next? A shift in belief occurred, which led to a plethora of runners conquering this once "impossible" feat. Today, thousands of people have done it. I don't believe humans evolved at such a rapid rate in the 50s and thus allowing our muscle fibers to increase in density, enabling new increases in speed and longevity. The only factor that changed was the belief that is was possible - starting with Roger Bannister, believing in himself and not allowing a commonly held belief to hold him back.

What you think about most, what you focus on, what you believe, has a direct connection to your overall well-being, happiness, and success.

Beliefs form our view on life, and nobody wants a blurry view. Our beliefs naturally guide us in the direction we most desire, and the clearer we are, the better the results. Our subconscious can be our best friend or our worst nightmare, and proper programming (via our thoughts and beliefs over time) is required. Put garbage in, get garbage out.

Developing clarity is one of the hardest things to do; we are very complex creatures and knowing oneself thoroughly is not easy. I was always the kid trying to do anything and everything because I never knew what I wanted out of this life. I would tell my mom, "If I knew what I wanted to do, I would start now and be the best at it!" - I was 12 years old. Sure, I held the empowering belief I could do anything and be great at it, but unfortunately, I had nowhere to point this energy.

My goals and aspirations were fuzzy at best.

Let's look at a better example, from a person who knew what he wanted to do and the value he believed he was worth...

Picture the story of Canadian born Jim Carrey, rising from being a small time comedian in Ontario, and landing on the big screens all over the world. Want to know something special about him? As crazy as he portrayed himself on screen, Jim had clarity - he knew what success meant to him and he believed he had the ability to capture it. Do you have this kind of belief in yourself? This is what he had to say:

"I wrote myself a check for ten million dollars for acting services rendered and dated it Thanksgiving 1995. I put it in my wallet and it deteriorated. And then, just before Thanksgiving 1995, I found out I was going to make ten million dollars for Dumb and Dumber. I put that check in the casket with my father because it was our dream together." ~ Jim Carrey. He knew his value, he believed in himself, and even put a deadline on it! Do your dreams have deadlines? Do you possess the beliefs in yourself to back them up?

GREAT ROLE MODELS

Did you know that Michael Jordan was dropped from his high school team? He believed in himself, he believed he could fly, and before we all knew it he was flying across the NBA courts.

Lance Armstrong believes that winning is about heart, not just the legs. Your heart has to be in the right place. He also believes that if you are worried about falling off the bike, you'd never get on.

When Tiger Woods was a young boy, he wrote down on a 3x5 card that he was going to break all of Jack Nicklaus' records. Look at him now. Jack Nicklaus agrees that Woods can do it if he stays on the track he's on.

Bill Gates believes in the importance of hard work, and if you are intelligent and know how to apply your intelligence, you can achieve anything. This led him to drop out of college (scary!) to follow his passions.

Will Smith believes, "I can create whatever I want to create," and "We are who we choose to be". Pretty powerful beliefs, right?

All these people started with a belief and moved on to greatness. They believed in themselves and it's easily visible with everything they do. You shouldn't have to build confidence in yourself by the accomplishments you achieve, you should achieve accomplishments by the confidence you have in yourself.

WHAT PREVENTS SUCCESSFUL BELIEFS?

Have you failed more often than not? Have you been told by people close to you, that you won't amount to anything? What is holding you back from holding successful beliefs?

That last question may sound silly because why would anyone hold onto beliefs that are not beneficial to themselves? Ludicrous! Well, this tends to be the main problem that people have because belief formation is not dependent on a logical framework and are extremely resistant to logical thinking.

Our Universe is made up with so much potential and resources. Salespeople know that in order to get what you want in life then you must possess these resources. The most powerful resources they possess is presence and strong belief.

Why would a person believe they can't do something if they have no past experience in which to base that belief? Isn't it just as easy to believe you can do something? It sure is, but usually fear finds a way to sneak in and blind us. That is what is so great about fear - fear is usually a red flag, an indicator for opportunities to grow. If our beliefs create our reality then in order to change our reality, we must first change our beliefs. Let's look at how we can do that.

AFFIRMING HEALTHY BELIEFS

Affirming concise and palatable beliefs refer to consciously programming your brain with positive thoughts. Reminding yourself of the potential you possess, the feelings you want to experience, the life you expect to have, and the life you want to live.

I suggest creating your own affirmations that are personal to you in which you can easily subscribe to. Affirmations could include:

"I am a successful, hard-working, and motivated businessman who people trust, respect and love doing business with."

"I am a loving father and husband who shows love, affection, and encouragement to my wife and children."

"I get excited and joyful when an opportunity arrives to help someone."

"I feel energized when a challenge presents itself because it is just one more success waiting to happen."

"My life is filled with an abundance of opportunities waiting to be acted upon."

"My mind and body are clean and healthy and I do something everyday to ensure this."

"I can do anything I set my mind to."

The most powerful statements are the ones that start with "I am..." because you are declaring your ideal image of yourself and your brain will start aligning itself with this image as if you've already become that person.

Sometimes affirmations don't feel like they fit, or we aren't living up to the expectation of the affirmation, and that is fine.

If you are new to the idea behind affirming healthy beliefs then it may feel like you are lying or tricking yourself into believing something that isn't true. Affirmations are not meant for lying to ourselves; their purpose is to enable the potential within us to fulfill the affirmations. Affirmations help fight the fear that holds us back from the action.

In order for my concious mind to accept my affirmations, I generally start them out with, "I allow…", "I accept…", "I welcome", or "I choose." For example, I allow myself to get married to an amazing person. Or, I accept owning my first home. And by using these starters it makes it easier for your mind to accept them.

But your mind is prone to rejecting anything that isn't habitual so if you hear your mind coming back and saying, "This isn't true" then softly say to yourself, "Got it and thank you for sharing." And resume affirming your new healthy beliefs.

Through affirmations, we consciously note the person we want to become, and we actively move in the direction naturally by programming our thoughts and beliefs. Simply thinking the affirmation does not have a positive effect until it is repeated, believed, and felt. This has the potential to be powerful. Start thinking of your subconscious brain as a programmable entity and you'll start aligning your thoughts and beliefs to promote feelings you want to experience.

START HAVING SUCCESSFUL BELIEFS

Personally, I strongly believe that men/women should have a life filled with creating - creating ideas or inventions, creating a better world, creating value for others, and creating a fulfilled life. In doing so, you leave your unique mark on the world.

I believe if you don't have the discipline to convert thought and beliefs into action, you are not living successfully. This belief pushes you and motivates you to produce something on a regular basis giving you feelings of accomplishment, satisfaction, and joy for fulfilling your belief.

If I don't, I feel I am not living up to my potential. I don't even have to push myself anymore, I simply have the drive, urge, and need to create something.

To start having successful beliefs, we need to start by recognizing the ones that hold us back, and as we noted, beliefs are not bound by logic. How can we pinpoint these harmful beliefs? We can do this by making goals and recognizing thoughts that arise when we aim big. We can do this by looking at our previous track record and discovering why we failed or succeeded. Sometimes other people have to tell us. And many times, recognizing a negative belief is as simple as listening to yourself every time you use the words, "I can't...".

Eliminate these negative beliefs by questioning them and start creating beliefs that motivate you to action, push you to succeed, remind you of your purpose, and fires up your confidence. The battlefield to success is not in the world, it's inside your head. Figure that out and the world changes in front of your eyes.

Most of us hold ourselves back by some of the beliefs we hold, we place restrictions and limitations upon ourselves. This is normal because that's what we're taught or our mind habitually adopted this belief because of repitition. We once believed that light not produced by the sun or fire was impossible. Thanks, Edison. We once believed human flight was impossible. Thanks, Orville and Wilbur Wright. Successful people hold successful beliefs, isn't it about time everyone joined in?

THINK ABOUT IT:

What beliefs do you hold that push you to reach new levels of success?

What beliefs do you hold that limit you from reaching new levels of success?

Look in the mirror, how do you feel about yourself?

Close your eyes, what do you think about yourself?

Do you believe you'll be successful?

How do you feel about money and its role in success?

Do you have reasons for why you are not successful? Try and debunk these.

Do you make a failure into a success by learning from it?

Are your beliefs shaped by fear and uncertainty?

Do you believe you can make a difference but fail to act?

What belief is holding you back?

Dig deep and get to know your beliefs. You have to discover a belief you hold before you can change or upgrade it.

What feelings arise when I think about something I want to/plan to do? Beliefs lead to the feelings we experience so knowing our feelings can lead to understanding our belief!

CHAPTER FIVE

Building Self Confidence To Make Your Dreams A Reality

Few people truly succeed in life. A vast majority of people are withdrawn and shy - they don't have many friends, as they are unable to interact meaningfully with people outside of their inner-circle. Boys don't find dates easily and girls fail to impress, all because of their lack of self-confidence. Can you tolerate a speaker whose utterances do not carry conviction? Timid speakers don't captivate their audiences. They can't be persuasive. In short, their speeches don't have the necessary pep and spirit to be exciting and end up falling flat. Timid people continue through life somehow, but as they don't stand up to be counted, success is something they only dream about. Why not go for it? A lack of self-confidence is what keeps most from being assertive, successful and ultimately happy in life. However, if you can recognize that you lack the self-confidence you want, you can work on building it up and making your dreams of success a reality.

If you can recognize the qualities of a person brimming with self-confidence, this will help you succeed in building your self-confidence. How do you know that a person is confident? It's easy, really. If you are balanced and confident, you are assertive, your body language conveys your confidence, you hold your head high, you speak with authority but not with arrogance, your attitude is positive, you go after your goals with determination - well-prepared to overcome any hurdles en route because you don't flinch at taking calculated risks whenever required, and whenever you make mistakes, you readily and graciously own up to them. Like people with low self-confidence, you don't look for scapegoats in such circumstances. Like people who are over-confident, you don't allow yourself to make those mistakes too many times. And unlike people with no confidence at all, you are outgoing and courageous. Your goals are set realistically, keeping in mind a fair assessment of your assets, your weaknesses and your skills and talents. On the other hand, over-confident people, as you may observe, have a tendency to set unreachable goals and prone to be hurt and have their confidence shattered when failure stares them in the face.

BUILDING SELF-CONFIDENCE

While attempting to build self-confidence, you may have a couple of questions to ask yourself. Is it possible to build self-confidence? If by nature you are not initially endowed with confidence, you may think you stay that way forever. Not necessarily. You can actually take small but reachable steps in order to build good confidence. However, self-confidence and success are interdependent. Normally, you can't succeed without confidence playing a role in your efforts and without success you can't have self-confidence.

If that is the case, how do you build self-confidence? Good question. Start by setting yourself a small enough goal that you can achieve it without too much difficulty. Then achieve it and watch your confidence grow. Repeat the steps, every time making the goal a little tougher than before and gradually build your confidence step by step.

SECRETS TO BUILDING SELF-CONFIDENCE

The first secret of building self-confidence is to honestly analyze your strengths and weaknesses. The next one is to work hard on minimizing the weaknesses while maximizing your strengths. I am stating minimizing weakness in the sense of knowing what they are and how they can prevent you from getting what you want. By no means am I saying work on your weakness because that will not work unless it feels with a skill set you are trying to attain. Arm yourself well with good, solid preparation to make the most of the opportunities available to do the job and to do it as best as you possibly can. Also, shield yourself against any anticipated threats that might stop you or slow you down in your tracks.

Time management is of utmost importance in all your efforts. Training yourself mentally is also equally important. The better your analysis, training, and preparation, the better your chances of success and the stronger your self-confidence. Build it to the appropriate levels and achieve success in all aspects of your life.

BUILDING SELF-CONFIDENCE WITH SELF-BELIEF

Do you realize that building self-confidence is in direct proportion to how much self-belief we have for ourselves and in everything that we set out to do? We come up against many obstacles in life, starting from early childhood and the obstacles become larger as we grow older.

It is a question of how we deal with them and as we reach adulthood, there are some decisions that can define how successful or unsuccessful we become. In all areas of life and occupations, it is our self-belief that will create our destiny.

When our self-belief is strong, our confidence rises and when our self-belief falters, then our confidence ultimately dwindles. The hard part about building our self belief is that we have a limited view of ourself which is constantly being reinforced by daily activities and experiences. Expanding your beliefs is the way to build a stronger self belief. I have attended and listened to countless personal growth programs not to mention the numerous assignments that I have done. They all played a part in me building an unshakable self-belief and has boosted my self confidence tremendously.

You only have to look in areas of achievement, like sport, where in some cases the odds are stacked against the competitor, where they fail time and time again, but still, have the self-belief and spirit to keep going and have that "never say die" attitude.

They refuse to give up and look at failure as just another step on the road to success. The same can be said about other groups of individuals who are impaired by disabilities, but they find an inner strength and belief to accomplish near impossible feats.

Building self-confidence in these two examples is not an option, because they have it in abundance. Their self-belief is so strong and unwavering, that their confidence remains high at all times.

By having the determination, persistence and focus to achieve, we can also have that same self-belief. Without it, the aim of building self-confidence and making it a reality will never happen.

Are you ready to start believing in yourself? What are you passionate about? What do you love doing? Are you ready to make a difference in your life? These are questions you need to ask yourself and let your self-belief raise your confidence to new heights.

Leave the past behind and make a fresh new start. Believe you are capable of anything you want to achieve. Decide on what you are going to pursue and don't give up until you achieve it. Let your confidence soar and make it happen. It all starts with that five inches between your head!

Don't let setbacks defeat you. We all have them, it is a part of life and it is how you deal with them that is important. Look at failure as a step nearer to success. If Thomas Edison would have given up, there would have been no light bulbs. He failed his way to success!

Set your sights on the finishing line and have the belief to achieve your dreams. There is something remarkable about self-belief that feels like magic. You feel in control of all that you do. You have the confidence to take the next step in everything that you do, without fear or hesitation.

When self-belief is missing, you don't seem to want to make a choice, because fear takes over and more often than not, opportunities are missed. This is a result of lacking self-confidence, which stems from the lack of self-belief.

Your mind can only receive one thought at a time, so hold that thought of self-belief, that anything is possible and don't let any negative thought take its place, and when it does, be willing to question the thought.

When you wake up in the morning, think about what you want to achieve each and every day. If you falter in your daily tasks, don't beat yourself up about it, it is a learning curve that you need to move forward.

At the end of each day, maybe when you go to bed, reflect on what you have achieved for that day and be happy in the knowledge that you are showing the attributes of inner self-belief to even think in this way.

You are building self-confidence and when you start to believe in yourself, others will believe in you as well.

BUILDING SELF CONFIDENCE THAT ENDURES

What would you do if you knew you could do anything? Imagine turning your dreams into reality. If you have a dream and you want to see it come to pass, then it's time to starting developing your confidence. Where do you start? How about with knowing what confidence is in the first place.

Take a look at its definition and see if this describes you: belief in oneself and one's powers and abilities; assurance. If that doesn't sound like you, then let's start right where you are right now. There are certain things you do every day that you know that you know you can do. Right? You believe in yourself in that area of your life.

Since you do have a success track record in a certain part of your life, then you have what it takes to build on it. Success breeds success. You are going to discover what works best for you and take your revelation and apply to making your dreams come true.

You must have 3 things you use on a daily basis that must agree with one another in order for you to build confidence that will sustain you through the trials.

1. *Your words.* When you listen to successful, confident people you can tell they are determined and optimistic they are going to accomplish their goals. Take a quick word inventory right now. Are you saying what you want? Are your words taking you in the direction of your dream? If not, start today to line your words up with your dream.

2. *Your beliefs.* Your confidence will grow when you have beliefs that align with the direction you want to go in life. How are your beliefs formed? What you see, hear, read and do all play a significant factor in developing your belief system. What you allow in your heart will determine what comes out of it. This week, pay special attention to what you are seeing and hearing.

3. *Your actions.* What you do is a reflection of what you are saying and what you believe you can and cannot do. If you do not see yourself do what you've always wanted to do, then you are not going to take the necessary

actions. This one step here is going to require you to take a step of faith.

Every time you take a faith step, it builds your confidence. Are you playing it safe or are you living on the edge and living by faith? One way will keep you from what you desire to do and the other will guide you in the right direction.

You have been given an awesome gift. It's called free will. You get to choose what you say, believe, and do. Today is the day you can start building your confidence so you can live the life you're meant to live. The choice is up to you.

SECRETS FOR MAKING YOUR DREAMS A REALITY

"If one advances confidently in the direction of his dreams and endeavors to live the life which he has imagined, he will meet with success unexpected in common hours." ~ Henry David Thoreau

Do you feel helpless in the process of making your dreams a reality? Do you get confused with choosing the best route for your success? Would you rather just give up altogether on the whole dream-chasing process?

It can be so frustrating when you want to make your life better but you don't really know how to get started. I want to share a few of the strategies that will give you the mindsets and the habits for your success. Achieving our dreams is a lot easier with these principles.

1. *Figure out what you don't want.* Don't begin with the overwhelming process of mapping out your dream. This can really bog you down. Identify the things you don't want in your life anymore. What would you like to see different? What are the things you are tired of? What is making you unhappy? This list can be quite long and may include things like:

"I don't have time for my family." "I'm fat and out of shape." "I never have time for me anymore." "I can't remember the last time I took a vacation." "I always have more bills at the end of the month than I do money." "I am tired of having a boss that doesn't appreciate me." I don't make enough sales in my business."

Let your mind think of as many complaints as possible because this will motivate you and help you to figure out the next step.

2. *What do you want?* Look at your above list and come up with a clearly defined statement or statements of what you truly want. Define who you want to be and what you want to accomplish. This can be a

scary step because we project what we want based on how we have been taught to think. And now you are beginning to change your thinking and self belief, you can encounter friction and fear. This is uncharted territory for most people who have gotten to this point because their old habitual mind pulls them back into safety. To have the courage to say and write exactly what you want to do. In my process of building self-confidence to live my dreams, it took me almost three years to really accept what I truly wanted to do. I battled with myself the whole time.

Clarity gives you strength and will help you build a sense of momentum. Most people are wishy-washy and this double-minded thinking only creates an avoidance of ever getting started in the first place. Write down what you want with power and conviction.

"I allow myself to be a great spouse and parent." "I am in excellent shape." "I am my own boss and I have an extremely successful business."

Once you write down what you want, things start to change.

3. *You don't have to be perfect to get started.* Thomas Fuller said, "A good garden may have some weeds." You have to start somewhere. If you wait until you're perfect, you will never begin. Everything is a process. You tap the piano keys for the first time. Next, you're playing a bit choppy. After a while of persevering practice, you are playing for friends at a sing-a-long. Be patient with yourself, but get started...Today!

4. *Spend more time on your dream.* "Every man is the architect of his own fortune." ~ Roman censor Appius Claudius Caecus

If you want more, you need to be willing to do more. Most people are not willing to do more. They will complain and talk negatively about how life has treated them unfairly. If you want more, you have to do the things that most people will not do. This may include waking up earlier or going to bed later or this may mean less television and more reading. Your willingness to make a sacrifice for your self-improvement will catapult you to a higher level of fulfillment. What I like about the personal sacrifice is what I become through the process of self-mastery and discipline.

"Nature gave men two ends - One to sit on, and one to think with. Ever since then, man's success or failure has been dependent on the one he has used the most." ~ Robert Albert Bloch.

> 5. *Stop worrying about everybody else.* "I cannot give you the formula for success, but I can give you the formula for failure, which is - try to please everybody." ~ Herbert Bayard Swope

I guarantee you that somebody is not going to like your dream, even if it is a wonderful goal that will improve the lives of mankind. Someone will have something negative to say about your dream. Often, it may be our own family. The people who love us the most can be the hardest to get support from. It may be that they are just watching out for us, but if you are not careful, they will steal your dream. Before long, you will be right back where you started, unhappy and tired.

Your business is to only sell your dreams to yourself- nobody else. As long as you make this the priority, you will win.

> 6. *Make a total commitment.* Commitment is the difference between success and failure. Your success lies not in the stars or with good luck but with your commitment. How bad do you want your dreams? You must have a will to succeed. Andrew

Carnegie said, "The wise man puts all his eggs in one basket and watches the basket." You will accelerate your progress once you gain the power of a concentrated focus.

7. *Expect to succeed.* "Someone's always saying, it's not whether you win or lose, but if you feel that way, you're as good as dead." ~ James Caan

Get excited about your dreams. Think about the outcome. See the achievement as if it has already occurred. Go ahead and feel the smile that comes from knowing you did it! Emerson tells us that, "Nothing was ever achieved without enthusiasm." You are the designer of your future. You have two choices; either the current path or a path of fulfillment. Neither path is harder than the other, but one brings consequences while the other gives benefits. So, make a decision right now to make your dreams come true.

CHAPTER SIX

You And God: The Premise

The experience of God is often hard-won. Attention and desire will activate the conditions for spiritual growth that will enable you to meet such goals. A simple place to start your search is in your dreams, a place where your sensors are down and revelation can more readily touch the heart of you.

I have a friend who is caught up in some serious "paralysis of analysis" where her business life is concerned. I advised her to simply follow God's peace and just get moving! She looked at me like I had suggested that she jump off a cliff. I could tell that she was literally frozen by her own fear of missing God.

Missing God is just not something that I've ever worried about. What do I mean when I say "I'm afraid of missing God?" anyway? It is as though some believe that God has set up a maze for them to figure out and if they go the wrong way - they've blown it and will be stuck in some dead end. I don't believe for a minute that God is like that.

God created you with unique talents and motivations. He put you together in a way that you would enjoy doing some things more than others. I believe that what you enjoy doing will give you a large clue about what you are called to do - whether that is in ministry, business or even a hobby.

We should be following our heart's desire when it comes to choosing a business. It should fit us like a glove and cause us to stretch and grow in our skills and our personal relationship with God. (As a business grows, our reliance on God for every decision will grow too!)

My friend told me that she fears that she can't tell what part of her desire is "just her" and what part of it is "God". I understand the fear of doing something in the flesh - but I don't think that spirit-filled salespeople who earnestly desire to please God need to worry so much about splitting spiritual hairs over their interests and desires.

Is the desire good? Will it suit your gifting and lifestyle? Will it fit well with your family? Can you do it and bring honor to God? If you can answer yes to all that, it's good!

Is the desire bad? Is there anything unethical or illegal about it? Will it cause you to abandon and forsake your family? Will it cause you to do things that will dishonor God? If you can answer no to all that, it's good!

Discerning whether something is good or bad is not difficult! So why do we worry so much about whether a desire is "just from me"?

God gives us the desires of our heart. Think of that in two ways. Remember, God, put you together - so, in truth, He knew that the way He created you, you would have this creativity, this desire to stretch and grow and build. You could say that He put those desires in your heart from the beginning.

So when we feel those desires - and what we desire is good - we don't have to worry that what we desire isn't from God. I just accept that I am being drawn to the future that He has called me to.

That doesn't mean that we shouldn't bathe certain decisions in prayer. Yes - we do need to pray over certain choices we make. We need to turn to God for guidance on everything -, especially for timing. We all know what it is like to try to make something happen before God has ordained it - it's frustrating!

Rather than getting lost in a cloud of confusion, just take your dreams and desires to God.

"God, I feel very drawn to start this business (develop this partnership, release this new product, launch this new service, etc). I don't want to do anything outside of your will and timing. If I'm missing something, if this is a bad move for me - please close every door. I just lift my ideas up to you and ask you to give me a sense of peace when and if it's time to move ahead. Amen."

Such a simple prayer! You don't have to stop the prayer there though... snuggle up in a comfortable spot and just share your dreams and visions with God. Tell Him what you would do, where you would do it. Who you would do it with. Just pour it all out and then take time to listen.

He will give you feedback! You'll find that your vision will sharpen in these times - and you'll just know what does and doesn't belong.

And be flexible to changing how things look and turn out. It will never be finite to how you envision it so be open to this fact.

Once you've shared your vision with God - just follow peace.

Any area of confusion or frustration should be taken as a sign that it isn't the right timing, person, place or situation for you to move ahead with. Where there is peace - pursue it! Anytime you're just not sure - wait for that peace.

If you trust God and keep taking your vision back to Him in prayer - you won't get caught up in anymore paralysis of analysis. You'll be moving toward God's best for you - He promised!

HOW TO ACHIEVE WHAT YOU WANT OUT OF LIFE?

It is important to live your dream and not your nightmare. My definition of a living a nightmare is, living a life that is the opposite of fulfilled. It is living a life that is not satisfying, and living a life with constant regret and "I wish I would have done that." But I have great news! It is not too late for you to begin to live the life you deserve to live.

One thing that helped me begin to live the life that I deserve to live was to give myself permission to achieve my dreams.

Often, a person may feel like he or she doesn't have the right to achieve his or her dreams. This is because he or she has so much other responsibility, spouse, family, work, etc.

But the only thing that mindset does is put you at the back of the line. This means that you are putting everyone else and everything else before you. Now, it is a reality that many of us have other obligations, but the point is to balance your life.

When you balance your life, you are still able to fulfill your other obligations while working on things that are important to you as well. The same energy and passion you put into your other responsibilities, you should also put into something that is beneficial for your future.

So many times we get bogged down with other responsibilities, and before we know it we have stopped dreaming. And have just settled for not achieving what it is we desire to achieve. This is not fair to anyone. It is not fair to those who believe in you, and it most certainly is not fair to you.

It is not just enough to give yourself permission to dream. You have to also give yourself permission to reach your dreams and experience them. Everyone has a dream, but not everyone is working toward getting them out of their mind, and into reality. If your dream is just stuck in your mind then it is not helping anyone.

If you think back to when you were a child, were you fired up about your dreams? I know I was. Were you excited, and energized just by the mere thought that you could achieve them? Sure, you were. That was our mindset when we were children.

We had that "anything is possible" mentality. We thought that nothing was impossible to achieve. We eagerly shared our dreams with others. Even though we had no clue how they were going to happen. We had the faith that they would happen.

Now, what happens as we get older? Life happens, and people happen. I mean that somewhere in-between being a child who was destined to reach his or her dreams, and adulthood, things have happened in life to maybe slow us down, create a challenge or obstacle, or just caused us to settle for never achieving our dreams.

Another thing that I think happens is people. Yes, people happen. This means the "childlike faith" is no longer there because somewhere along the road someone said that it could not be done. And we allowed that fear of failure to set in and cause us to be stagnant, and not work toward achieving our dreams.

It is sad when we allow people to kill our dreams, destroy our dreams and delay our destiny. I have had my share of naysayers; but I had to make it up in my mind that what God said I could do, overrode what anyone said that I could not do.

That allowed me to develop an unstoppable mindset. I am empowered by faith to reach my dreams. I don't depend on my own ability, but I let God strengthen me to keep going, not give up, and achieve results.

I have had so many things up against me in life. My sister passed away tragically, I was a statistic of the real estate market crash in the late 2000's which left me broke, and a business partnership fell apart just a few months later. So I truly know how it feels to have challenges rise up against your dreams. But you have to realize that God created you to live a fulfilled life. He created you to reach your dreams. He created you to persevere, even in the face of adversity.

Many people ask me, "How did you do it?" I simply respond, I never let quitting be an option. Now, I didn't say that I didn't want to give up, but I knew that I had to keep going because on the other side of my pain was my purpose.

And God's grace allowed me to gain understanding of my true self and point me to who and what I truly am. And by doing so, I began a different course in life that now rings about peace, truth, and fulfillment.

As I am writing this chapter and reflecting back on my life, I know that there is no way that I would have made it if I was depending on my own ability. I thank God constantly that He blessed me to reach my dreams. And I am still working on things that I want to achieve.

I knew that if I didn't fulfill my dreams, someone may be missing out on something I have to offer. I knew that if I didn't fulfill my dreams I would not be able to share with others how God blessed me to persevere and prosper. So many times our journey is not just about us. But it is about others that we are meant to touch. It is time for you to unleash your dreams. And yes, I mean unleash. Just because you haven't thought about your dreams lately, does not mean they are not still there. Just because you have them tucked away safely in your past thinking, does not mean that they don't exist.

I have a life principle that I live by called Problem Solved. Anytime you are up against something that's difficult or you truly desire, I communicate my wants to God and say, "Problem Solved." From then on, my only job is to act in accordance that it has been done. And to take any inspired action when necessary to experience my desires.

It is realistic that you can achieve your dream. I believe in you, God believes in you, now you just have to believe in you.

If you have a feeling that there is more to your life than what you are currently experiencing, there is a great chance that your dreams are trying to get your attention. Are your dreams talking to you? What are they saying? Probably "Go for it. You deserve it!" How will your actions respond? Are you going to take action and go for your dreams? Or are you going to look back a year from now, still thinking that it is unrealistic that you can achieve them?

What do you want to say about yourself 1 year, 3 years, or 5 years about what you have done and accomplish. Start now- there is no time to waste. God supports you 100% in everything that you desire.

If you feel good when you think about your dreams, then imagine how great you will feel when you achieve them! Now, it is time to get started. So take action. You will be glad that you did!

UNLOCKING YOUR DREAMS AND LIVING YOUR DESTINY!

All dreams are birthed from our hearts and require faith, hope, love, and passion to see them accomplished.

What do you have faith for?

Whom do you have hope for?

What and whom do you love?

What's the passion burning inside of you?

Close your eyes for a moment and imagine a staircase before you. This staircase represents your dreams and the steps God will use to take you higher. It's a staircase of opportunity, of hope, of destiny, and of desire - a staircase flooded with God's favor, blessing, and anointing to allow you to reach the heights of all that God has for you.

Go on then, close your eyes and imagine the staircase God puts in front of you!

What do you see? Are you surprised at all? Did He show you more than you have ever dreamed? Did the staircase look incredibly high and impossible to climb? If so, good! You're dreaming God-sized dreams!

So, are you ready to start climbing your staircase or have you begun already?

Yes... no... maybe? Wherever you are on the journey, it's important to take a moment to stop and make sure you are approaching your staircase with wisdom, discerning what you desire to conquer, so that you can climb your staircase with excellence, prepared and organized for what lies ahead.

"If people can't see what God is doing, they stumble all over themselves; but when they attend to what He reveals, they are most blessed."

We don't want to stumble up our staircase, stubbing our toes on each step (obstacle) but rather climbing with grace; ready to run up when He calls us to.

TO UNLOCK YOUR DREAMS:

See the big picture and imagine your staircase

What &whom are you going after? Can you see it? Can you see them? What lives do you impact and how will you impact them?

- Can you discern what God has been stirring in your heart?

- What patterns or places have you always been drawn to?

- What people group do you continually pray for?

- What profession do you long to be in?

- What hobby brings you alive?

- What are those dreams that keep you up at night?

Have you hidden your dreams in a box to be locked up and never touched again?

"Click. Click. Click." God unlocks your box today! The words "I can't," "I won't," or discouragement from others will no longer hold you back. God is known for making something out of nothing, just look at the earth around you. Your Creator is the God of the possible, and He calls you today to dream again. He believes in you! He doesn't hold the past as a mark against you. Instead, He has grace for you today. He has hope for you today. He has joy for you today.

He has a destiny that lies before you and awaits your movement. He calls you into more today, and He asks, "Will you join me on this crazy ride?"

When doubt and fear come into your mind, He says, "come to me, I will show you my vision, I will show you how much I believe in you. Doubt and fear aren't of Me, I am the God of Heaven on Earth, who wants good things for you!"

You cannot out-dream God, so dream bigger and ask for more!

What God-sized prayers would you put before Him today? What burdens your heart? When you are 90 and looking back on your life, what do you want to have accomplished? What great work do you want to be written in the history books of time?

Today is the day where history-makers are made and dreams are birthed. Today, we stand with Rosa Parks, Dr. Martin Luther King, Jr, and the Saints before us who pursued the dreams in their heart and said, "I will not give in any longer."

Now, it's your turn. It's your day to stand in front of YOUR staircase and start climbing!

Meditate on all the questions above, and ask God to search your heart and show you what He made you specifically for. When you are ready, finish the sentence below.

I have a dream that one day...

"Every great dream begins with a dreamer. Always remember, you have within you the strength, the patience, and the passion to reach for the stars to change the world."
-Harriet Tubman

CHAPTER SEVEN

Choosing God's Will Over All Else

LOVE YOURSELF, ACCEPT YOURSELF

This type of thinking makes the ego feel secure and satisfied. Self-acceptance and real joy will not come about. Isn't life about being yourself?

Miracles remind us that your own uncertainty about what you must be is self-deception on a scale so vast; its magnitude can hardly be conceived. To accept yourself love yourself, is the chosen direction you take that is real. What really is a choice? It can only reflect some uncertainty as to what you are.

As you practice self-acceptance by asking for spiritual guidance and hearing the Voice of God, you will have no questions about your oneness because there is no thought, other than the One Thought that sustains you.

Where there is no choice, there is no doubt that can deeply root itself. It's awakening to the Light of Who you are. It is knowing the answer to, "What am I?"

"What or who am I?" How could you even be able to ask yourself this question, except for the fact that you don't recognize yourself? Only refusing to accept yourself as you are could make this question be bothersome to you.

Going within is where you will accept atonement, or we may say "Awakening". Yes, it's bringing the Light of truth to illusion and where inner conflict made by falsehood fades away.

To accept yourself love yourself, is the undoing of our separated thought system called ego which thinks we are separate from God. The Atonement is where you will witness it happening. How is it that you accept Atonement? With this, there can be no conflict in the question:

"What or who am I?" In this alone, you've discovered freedom.

We may think or say things like, "I'm not meant to be a popular salesperson" or "I must be crazy to think that I could ever become a doctor."

The only thing that is surely known by any living thing is that it is what it is. You see other individuals, and certain animals, as who they are, but you struggle with yourself. Why the inner conflict and uncertainty?

Often, we have an insight knowing we're capable of a higher potential or self-acceptance of who we are or what our true purpose might be, but we are quick to doubt or put it off as fantasy.

When you come to a decision to let go of inner conflict and accept yourself love yourself as God created you, it happens.

Living your life less than your true potential is equal to believing that who you truly are-- the One Thought of God about you-- does not exist.

Remember, to accept yourself love yourself, certainly heals inner conflict.

Don't you truly light up when you see individuals elated, thrilled and all fired up? It often makes my day when I see people with self-acceptance on top of the world, even when they are up against overcoming challenges and are ready and eagerly willing to operate from within and move forward. Miracles may be more clearly realized through this exercise for prayer or meditation, and I like to repeat these words in meditation first thing in the morning before getting out of bed:

Perfection created me perfect. This how I accept myself.

The separated ego cannot accept yourself love yourself because it is too busy judging against your true being and denies its worth, so we decide that we do not know the only certainty by which we have been living.

How could we be alive without knowing the answer? Still, we may think we do not know. It is this "something else" that becomes the questioner of what that "something" is. Deep inside, we all know the truth of who we are. What are we doing when we ask ourselves, "Who am I"?

We are suggesting that we are not ourselves, and therefore have chosen to be something else.

Again, to accept yourself love yourself, is the clearing away or undoing of your separated thought system called the ego-based mind, which thinks you are separate from God.

If you can remember that to accept yourself love yourself is the chosen direction you take that is real, you will set yourself up for success in this world.

Only refusing to accept yourself as you are could make this question be bothersome to you.

ACCEPTING YOURSELF JUST AS YOU ARE

What would it take for you to simply accept yourself? Would something about you have to change? If you could, would you accept yourself without requiring any necessary changes? I did and it was one of the best decisions of my life.

Several years ago, I was meditating on what acceptance was and what it was not. I discovered a truth about acceptance that may surprise you. I found out the opposite of acceptance was NOT rejection. The opposite of acceptance is resistance. Whatever we choose to resist, we are choosing not to accept. The more I resisted certain areas of my life the longer they lingered. Once I chose to accept them as they were, they seemed to just leave without any resistance on my part.

For many decades, I wanted to be accepted by others and tried, what I thought, were ways for them to accept me.

I discovered I needed to accept myself just as I am before anyone else was going to accept me.

Another discovery I made recently was that there is one who has always accepted me. God has always accepted me simply because of WHO I am and not what I do. He also accepts you based on your identity and not your performance. Isn't that good news? Acceptance from God is His choice and He chooses to accept you and I simply based on who we are. He does not ask us to change in order for us to be accepted by Him. He just wants us to believe that He accepts us just as we are. If we don't accept this truth, it does not change the fact He accepts us unconditionally. In other words, whether you believe He accepts you or not, He still does accept you, as you.

Once I realized I was completely accepted by God, I no longer had to try to earn or deserve His acceptance of me. He freely accepted me not based on my performance. This life-changing truth set me free to accept myself just as I am without having to make any changes at all. I no longer had to resist myself, but instead, love and accept myself unconditionally. Hopefully, you will soon discover that acceptance does not mean that you have to like or approve of yourself based on what you do. You can right now accept yourself because of WHO you are. What is so amazing about that truth is who you are never changes. Think about that truth. Who you are never changes. Who God created you to be will always be consistent.

When you believe that God accepts you just as you are and you begin to accept yourself as is, then you will see a transformation in your relationships.

You will begin to accept others just as they are and in turn, you will see others start accepting you just as you are. You will not base your acceptance of others on their performance anymore. You will love and accept them because of WHO they truly are. The question is WHO are you? You will only find your true identity in God. He created you. He knows you better than yourself. He knows your true identity and you need to go to Him to find out who you really are in order to live the life you are meant to live.

Choosing to accept God's acceptance of you is incredible. Choosing to accept yourself just as you are is awesome. Choosing to accept others just as they are is life changing. Choosing to discover who you are right now is your responsibility. Do you want God to reveal to you who you really are? He is willing right now to show you the truth of who you truly are. Why not ask Him to show you how much He loves and accepts you? The choice is up to you.

HERE'S HOW TO START

Are you happy with yourself just the way you are? Do you accept yourself with all your shortcomings? Most people don't. For several reasons.

For instance, society holds certain standards that by their very nature are almost impossible to live up to. You're supposed to strive for the perfect job.

The perfect home. The perfect family. The perfect relationship. The perfect body.

When we compare ourselves to this mythical "ideal person" - it's no wonder we lack self-acceptance! We live in a society that demands comparison and contrast and competition. But we'll never measure up to the ideal standards of perfection; the ones set up by the unspoken rules of society. Thus we can never accept ourselves. It's a no-win situation:

1. Here's the perfect/ideal person...
2. You must compare yourself to this image...
3. Perfection, by definition, is impossible...
4. herefore, you lose!

What makes it even worse is that we rarely - if ever - question this situation. We've bought into the lie. We accept that we're unacceptable without ever really stopping to evaluate why.

Which is one of the main reasons we stay stuck in our present condition? Because if you don't accept yourself, what will be your motivation for change? Anger? Ridicule? Derision? Self-loathing?

Is that really the fuel you want to use to better yourself?

Here's another reason so few people have self-acceptance:

We forget we're always a work-in-progress. Because we're stuck in time. We tend to see ourselves as standing on a pinnacle, or a plateau, or sadly maybe even a trough. No matter the image, it still seems to be somewhat of a "concluding statement" about ourselves.

"I am the sum total of all I've been."

True. But that's also going to be true next week, next year, next decade. Because while we can look around us in the present, and we can remember the past; the future seems so unknown... so elusive... so unreal. We tend to believe the future doesn't exist. And it may never exist. All we know is the present and the past.

I may never change because "This is where I've ended up in life."

Guess what? You never end up anywhere in this life. Life is a process. Not a destination. It's not about your "place" in life - because your place is always changing. Or it should be. It better be. Life is like a river. A never-ending river.

Remember when the sixth-graders looked so big? Then you got to the sixth grade. Then it's the high school kids who looked so big, so cool, so mature. We compare ourselves to others who are more than we are. Without realizing we're on our own path to becoming more.

Self-acceptance makes it much easier to grow and change. Why? Because it gives us something positive to push off from. It gives us something solid to stand on as we reach for more.

The problem is, we often confuse contentment with complacency. We confuse satisfaction with settling. If I'm content and satisfied with who I am and where I am right now (which means I'm accepting myself) then I'm in a stronger position to achieve more.

If I'm complacent; if I've settled - then I'm not likely to do much of anything to change. And this state can be confused with self-acceptance, rather than what it really is - self-resignation.

Admitting who and what you are, admitting your accomplishments, and taking responsibility for them - strengthens you.

"Yes, I want more. Much more. But I'm willing to pause and reflect and be responsible for all I've done up till now."

Do that, and you'll be one step closer to accepting yourself. Plus, by looking for the good, you'll find and create more of it.

Self-acceptance does not come easy. You're up against a lot of negative programming. But reflecting on your accomplishments can be a starting point.

Even if you used to be on a peak, and now you're in a tough spot, there has to be some sort of silver lining. At the very least, you have a greater awareness of life.

Maybe you're ready to accept yourself on a deeper, more profound level. Maybe it's time to love yourself a little more and judge yourself a little less harshly. Maybe today is the day you begin to embrace self-acceptance.

Nobody else can stop you from accepting yourself.

There are a few factors I would encourage you to look at when dealing with the topic of acceptance:

First, get to know yourself and what you believe in. Ask yourself these questions: Who are you? What is important to you in your life? What do you believe? These may seem like simple questions, but you would be surprised at how many people have never asked them of themselves.

Second, check your integrity level. How honest are you currently with yourself? How honest are you with others? Do you always communicate your true desires and wants to others? What do you believe to be true about yourself? What are your goals? Do you honestly believe you can achieve your goals? Do you honestly feel you deserve them?

Third, look at your current acceptance level. Do you openly accept yourself? Do you like yourself? Do you accept others? What characteristics do you like about yourself?

Which ones would you like to change? Do you see a reason to love and accept yourself the way you are right now?

Fourth, embrace the fact that you are doing the best you can with what you have. I believe that people sincerely do the best they can with the knowledge and resources they have at the time, especially when they are honest, open, and accepting of themselves and others. Giving you a break and acknowledging yourself for doing a great job now is acceptance. Let go of desires to do better, be better, or be different. This will allow you to see others in the same light, enriching all of your existing relationships as well as future relationships.

Fifth, let go of any guilt that you may have. Guilt is a useless emotion. As far as love and acceptance are concerned; the emotion of guilt really holds no place. If you truly feel guilty about something, it is usually because you are not comfortable with a choice you have made. Instead of feeling the useless emotion of guilt, learn from the choices you have made and make different choices in the future.

Finally, understand your motivations. Understand your likes and dislikes about yourself. A desire to constantly grow, learn, and improve is honorable. Just make sure that you are simultaneously accepting and loving all areas of yourself, even the areas you want to change.

Relationships, where one or both parties aren't truly able to be themselves, are destined for failure. You will quickly realize that you can't live in-authentically. Your energy is so much better served if people are allowed to be themselves and love and grow together for who they are. Once you are able to master acceptance, you are well on your way to finding enriching, fulfilling relationships with all.

A SIX-STEP PROCESS

I see many people who have issues, habits or characteristics which may be frowned on by others. However, the way in which they express themselves endears you to them. This is because they have, at some level, accepted themselves for who they are. This process gives you a six-stage process that will teach you how to accept yourself so you can relax in your own skin and enjoy your life.

Accepting yourself means you are able to speak from a position of power, dignity, and pride. This makes you completely congruent and confident despite what others may think of you, and despite whether or not you are accepted by society. So in order to be able to accept yourself and feel comfortable in your own skin, follow this six-step process:

Stage 1. Articulate the issues preventing you from moving forward as if you're talking to a third party (e.g a professional, practitioner, therapist, customer or even a friend). This sometimes helps you to express the issues in a constructive manner, and in a way that keeps your dignity intact.

Stage 2. Decide what it is about yourself that you like and reinforce it. We all have parts of ourselves that we like. One way to root these out is to ask yourself the question: "Why am I glad I'm me?" Identify and list as many aspects here as you can. Once your list is drawn up, focus on your positive aspects, reinforce them and strengthen them daily.

Stage 3. Decide what you don't like about yourself, and set yourself on a path to improve those aspects that are important for you to address. Choose the aspects that prevent you from progressing and decide to improve just those.

Stage 4. For those other aspects you don't like about yourself, but you're willing to live with, decide to let go of the need to fix them. This is an important mindset shift as it frees you up from the need to change every downside, every fault or every negative trait about yourself.

Stage 5. This stage is about making the decision to fully accept yourself for who you are, what you are and where you are in life given your good and not so good points. Even though this may be easier said than done, it's not impossible. Self-acceptance is an extremely liberating point to get to as it allows you to let go, move on and live your life with authenticity and integrity.

Stage 6. The last stage is about finding as many ways as possible to communicate to others - with pride and from your inner core - who, what and where you are on your life journey. This ensures you're always congruent, true to yourself and able to maintain yourself respect and dignity. It is by going through the first five stages that makes this stage much easier.

Following this simple process will have a profound effect on your life. When, for instance, you're in situations in which you disagree with something that's been said, your self-acceptance, authenticity and integrity will prevent you from jumping in and concurring with the person just to avoid conflict.

CHAPTER EIGHT

God Is A Yes For Your Dreams And Desires, Launch Them

Would you like to experience a glorious life, bathed in riches that fill you to overflowing? Now is the perfect time to create this life as this year is launched. Isn't it exciting to realize this is a huge opportunity to bring into reality the dreams you've been dreaming for weeks, months, or perhaps even years?

What are your dreams? Are they something that you've had on the back burner for some time now, or perhaps you've all but abandoned them, deciding they can never come true since you cannot figure out how they could ever work. Ah! Here's the key to this entire saga of bringing dreams to fruition - forget trying to figure it all out!

Perhaps you have no real dreams. Maybe you've been sliding through life accepting what came your way as how it is meant to be. Did you ever actually sit down quietly and think about what you wish your life could look like? This is the first and most important step - defining what you truly want. You see, the Universe cannot bring you the desires of your heart unless you first have a wish and declare it. It is up to you to decide what you want in your life. We call this intention, a thought if you will, that comes from a deep desire in the heart. Take a few minutes right now (it's too important to put off), and make a visible list on paper of what you truly want in your life. Read it often, daily if you wish, keeping that desire alive because that is how your dreams will come to fruition.

What is on your list? Do they seem impossible to become reality? As long as you doubt, your dreams can come true, they probably won't. People are really good at self-sabotage. They place an intention of their desire, but then block the entire process by doubts, (negativity), often because they are trying to figure out how to make it happen instead of allowing the Universe to fulfill the dream. So this is step number two - Get out of the way! This is without a doubt a most difficult aspect of our lives - that of trusting the process to unfold in Divine timing without doing a single thing. Human beings, by nature, want to get in the middle and make it happen - control. Letting go of control - surrendering - is most difficult.

Many individuals are taught that in order to achieve anything you must work hard, head to the grindstone. You have probably been encouraged to set goals and take the steps to make them happen. This is stressful oftentimes and requires many grueling hours to complete. While it may bring the desired results, in the end, it takes a lot of pushing and driving to facilitate. However, when you have placed your intention of your desire, surrendered the whole process to God and stepped out of the way, amazing things will happen without any effort on your part. It is a most incredible process that of allowing Divine orchestration to unfold your plan as you patiently wait.

I have experienced this over and over in my life. It allows me to be at peace, knowing what I desire will happen for me according to the universal plan for my highest good. There have been multiple times when I had no idea how to accomplish what I wanted to do, but when I simply said, "Okay God, You take over," it worked out with ease in a way I would have never been able to orchestrate

Once a door opens for you, it is time to move - step number three. Now, it is time to begin working hard to fulfill this dream that is opening for you. This is the place that stops many people from moving forward because they must actually step up to the plate and do what they said they wanted to do. It can be frightening to step out into unknown territory, grabbing the reins for success, so sometimes people turn around and walk away, too afraid to continue with their dream. How sad. If they had only taken a moment to carefully contemplate, they might have realized that the universe doesn't open a door unless it is possible to achieve what is on the other side of that door. People are afraid of failure, so rather than risk failing, they turn away. This is so sad. All it would take is a little faith and belief in the power that resides within as a co-creator with the Creator of the Universe, and the fear could be eliminated.

Step number four reveals a core tool of empowerment - be thankful for the fulfillment of your dream before it shows up in your life. There is a universal principle that I feel sure you have heard about many times - what you focus on expands into more of the same.

If you are grateful for something, an expression of love, it will expand into more outcomes from love (positive). So it only makes sense to concentrate on something good so more good will come to you.

Being thankful before there is any evidence of your dream coming to fruition shows that you have faith and believe that God and the universe are listening and will deliver the desires of your heart as is promised. Faith - a belief in something not seen - is a powerful vibration that attracts back to it what is being sent out on the energy waves of that vibration.

So there you have it - four simple steps for bringing your dreams into your reality. Let's do a recap of these so they will be indelibly placed in your mind.

1. Decide what you want and place an intention of that desire to God and the Universe. You must define what it is you desire in order for the universe to bring it to you.

2. Surrender the process and step out of the way. It is easy and effortless when you do this, but often difficult since human beings want to control everything.

3. When an opportunity appears and a door opens, walk through it and begin working hard. This stops

many people since they are afraid of stepping up to the plate and actually doing it.

4. Be thankful for your dream coming to you before there is any evidence that it is coming.

This shows you have faith and belief in the power of God and the Universe to bring you your request.

So there you have it - the simple steps for launching your dreams into viable experiences that materialize into your actual life. But let me leave another thought with you about launching your dreams into your reality.

Be sure to dream big! So many people are afraid to dream big because they don't see how something so grand could materialize, so they opt for small dreams. I'm suggesting that you dream as big as you possibly can, and here are some questions to ask yourself so you know if your dreams are actually big enough.

1. Does my dream excite me?
2. Is my dream in alignment with my spiritual core?
3. Do I need help from God (Higher Power) in order for this dream to materialize?
4. Will this dream require me to grow beyond where I am at present?
5. Will my dream bless others at some point?

When you can answer "Yes" to all of these questions, your dream is big enough. My challenge to you, my friend, is to create your dreams and allow them to unfold so that your year is great!

CONCLUSION

We come into this world freely expressing ourselves, and then slowly but surely, our wings get clipped, as we are taught that "this is good", "that is bad", and if we want to fit into society we need to behave in a particular way or else we may get ostracized. As if that were not enough, many of those who go through some kind of religious upbringing, growing up with additional guilt complexes, because to live up to the ideal presented by a religion, people are often expected to deny and suppress their human nature, their human needs and desires and suppression always creates problems - first, mental and emotional, and eventually physical - because the suppressed energy needs to express in some way.

Being "holy" or "whole" implies inclusiveness. You cannot be and experience yourself as "whole" if you split yourself into bits and pieces and then reject parts of yourself as if they were not an integral part of you. Being "whole" implies embracing all of your energy, all that you have judged and labeled as "good" and wonderful about you and all that you may have judged and labeled as "bad" or undesirable. All those "good" and "bad" things are just energy.

When you reject parts of yourself because you have labeled them as "bad", your own energy, your own life-force, is vested in maintaining those parts, in pushing and suppressing that energy so that you wouldn't be aware of it, so that you wouldn't have to deal with it. You are using your energy to push them away, to hide them from yourself and others, because you don't know what to do with them. When you do this, it creates stress, pressure, inner conflict, anxiety, and guilt. It blocks the free flow of energy within you and in time creates mental, emotional and physical problems. It keeps away from you the experience of fully experiencing the joy of life, the experience of feeling an abundance of life-force freely flowing through you, freely expressing through you. When you block the free flow of energy within you, you feel tired, you age faster, you compromise your immune system, and you erect a barrier that prevents many wonderful things coming into your life.

When you embrace all of your parts, when you invite and welcome them, love them and accept them, regardless of how imperfect or undesirable you may have considered them to be, enormous energy becomes liberated within you.

With each part that you embrace, you are becoming free of some unnecessary burden, of baggage you have been carrying around, you begin to feel lighter, you can breathe easier, you feel more energized, you can accomplish more things, you have more energy to invest in creating the life you'd enjoy living, you feel good about yourself, you become healthier, and more importantly, you begin to experience inner peace.

When you include and integrate all that is part of you, there is no longer inner conflict, there is no more inner war, there is no more any friction within you that creates stress - there is only sweet peace.

When you look at your life, you may become aware of many things you did or said, that perhaps you wish you did or said in some other way. You may become aware of many errors you made you wish you didn't. You may become aware of all sorts of weaknesses and imperfections. And if you look around you, the great news is - we are all in the same boat. All of us have our own weaknesses and imperfections, all of us have done countless things we may wish we did differently. Have you ever met any perfect human being? I don't think so. It is ludicrous to expect perfection either from yourself or from others. And as long as you are living, and growing and learning new things, you can rest assured that you will make many more errors.

The only thing any of us can do, at any point in time is simply do our very best. If you commit yourself to doing your very best and accept and love all those parts of you that may need some polishing, just like one loves a small child, that is still growing and learning, you will live at peace with yourself and with the world. If you are aware of your own weaknesses and imperfections when you notice them in other people, you may have more compassion, toward yourself and toward other people.

If you embrace and accept your human nature, even while you are unfolding spiritually, if you let yourself be, instead of indulging in feelings of guilt, you will also lose the temptation to point fingers at others, you will let them be. People who tell others "you should be ashamed of this or that", are those who are burdened and tormented with feelings of guilt, hoping that if they can make someone else feel guilty, they could feel better about themselves, but they never do, until they learn to accept themselves just the way they are.

When you fully and completely accept yourself, then it won't matter what anyone else says or thinks about you, because you will be at peace with yourself. If you have accepted all that you have judged as "good" and "bad" about you and someone says that something you did was "bad", you can acknowledge that you could've done better, love yourself just the way you are, and if you feel that you need to change something about you, change when you are ready. You can take whatever action is appropriate without ever crucifying yourself for the errors you made. You can simply correct the errors that you can, move on with your life and keep on doing your best.

So, if you like take some time to welcome all those aspects of yourself that have thought, said or done things you may not feel so good or proud of. Embrace them as if they were your own little children. Call back any parts of you that you feel ashamed of, any parts of you that make you feel guilty, and embrace them.

And as you do, you may become aware that they are transforming and dissolving into pure energy and you are feeling more and more alive, free, expanded, happy and at peace. As you accept and love all of you, all that is part of your being and your life, you may discover that you have opened the door to miracles and many wonderful surprises. GOD REALLY LOVES SALES PEOPLE.

About The Author

Amani Ahmed is a national author & speaker who finds delight in the areas of self-awareness, human potential, and abundant living.

Having studied and researched self growth & spirituality for over 25 years, overcome her own rigorous mental, emotional, and life challenges, Amani knows what it takes to turn times of struggle into joy. Drawing from these insights, she has helped thousands of people create a life of everlasting value. In terms of her writings, Amani has unique style and welcoming approach which individuals tend to connect to instantly. Moreover she goes as far as understanding her clients and their limitations, helping them maximize their potentials, and unshackle them from destructive thinking.

A native born of the nation's capital, Washington D.C. to Egyptian parents. She finds balance in life through spiritual advising, reading, speaking, and learning new things about herself and life. Amani is a kid at heart who is curious about life and achieving personal success.

www.ingramcontent.com/pod-product-compliance
Lightning Source LLC
Chambersburg PA
CBHW031406040426
42444CB00005B/439